WORKaDAY

¤

Grey Held

FUTURECYCLE PRESS

www.futurecycle.org

Cover artwork, photocomposite by Diane Kistner of architectural photos (pexels.com); author photo by Patrick Singleton; cover and interior book design by Diane Kistner; Cronos Pro text with Audiowide and Alte Caps titling

Library of Congress Control Number: 2018963923

Published by FutureCycle Press
Athens, Georgia, USA

ISBN 978-1-942371-61-8

for Zachary and Jesse

Contents

1
Upward Progress to Measure Like a Stock Price

2
Business Trip to Düsseldorf

3
Business Trip to Las Vegas

4
Business Trip to Orlando

5

Business Trip to Richmond, Where I Grew Up

6

Re-Evaluation

7

Shaking Off My Expectations

*In the name of God, stop a moment, cease
your work, look around you.*

—Leo Tolstoy

*Someone first thought it:
an ox gelded, tamed, harnessed to plow.
Then someone realized the wooden yoke could hold two.
After that, mere power of multiplication.
Railroads, airplanes, factory ships canning salmon.*

—Jane Hirshfield

1

Upward Progress to Measure
Like a Stock Price

i. My Designated Parking Spot at Work

My front-end grillwork up against a chain link fence
on whose other side: a sumac,
    rooted in asphalt, gravel,
chips of bottle glass.

When I was entry level, that sumac was
a sapling, a handspan from that fence.

By the time I'd doubled the size of my client base,
    that sumac was sequencing its leaves,
foisting its clusters of wine-red berries into air,
    adding to its girth, ring by ring, closing in
on the mineral enterprise of that fence.

By the time I became the Manager,
    the fence had embossed itself into the sumac,
    so that the bark, in unfettered aggression,
could pilfer a section of gridlock.

ii. Memo From the CEO

My job is to economize,
     so I sell a lackluster division.
I say *good-bye* to the west coast
     sales director and his indecent margin;

good-bye to the payroll manager, because, well,
because she deserves it.
     I deserve the best
     leather swivel chair, the best

desk with a rosewood grain,
     a penthouse window, so the smallness of
the people on the street give my life a sense of
     scale. Sometimes I increase

incentives. Sometimes I cut commissions.
After all, I'm the CEO today, tomorrow, and
     for as long as interest rates are soaring.

iii. Executive Planning Room

I book the Executive Planning Room
that only vice-presidents and up can book.

Only we get to watch raindrops swagger down
        its panoramic glass.

The leather chairs are tarmac black.
Or is it Black Monday black?

Two walls are covered with white boards: vinyl, slimy.

Toxins in the markers and the capable erasers turn
        the next great idea into a smear.

The carpet is beige, unstainable, though I'd like to spill
        my cappuccino, and try.

When the blinds are closed, beware of layoffs.
Work is dangerous,

a turn-over system like commuting by train—
someone gets off, someone less
        expensive gets on.

iv. Smoking Area

In the cinder-blocked smoking area
behind the vending machines, it's just
Anton, me, and Basra from Somalia,
the new employee with a scar
from a machete on her lovely throat.

> *Summa cum laude* from Oxford,
> she's working the Global Economy
> on an American green card, telemarketing
> in the cubicle down the hall. Anton
> has worked the mail room for thirteen

years: sorting, metering, packaging,
measuring his waning Slavic accent
by the yardstick of democracy.
Lighting up a Parliament, he tells me
about his collection of coins from Yugoslavia.

> He takes from his pocket a shiny 1931
> ten *dinara*, places it double-headed
> eagle-side up in my palm. The metal is
> as old as the country he was minted
> in, the country that no longer exists.

v. Smoking

On the final day of the company-sponsored
Quit Smoking Class, I buy the 12-ounce jam jar
the teacher said to get, to empty out and clean,
so as to become the receptacle to put the butt

> of my good-morning cigarette in. Also the ten
> o'clock cigarette. The lunchtime cigarette.
> The mid-afternoon pick-me-up
> cigarette. The cocktail cigarette. The relax-
> after-sex cigarette. The dinner cigarette.
> The go-to-take-a-shower cigarette. The bed-
> time cigarette. The unsleepable wee-hour one,
> its nihilistic tip glowing bright, going out.

I will miss tobacco's sleek paper sleeve
between my fingers, the struck match,
the sudden sulfur flare against the flint.
I will miss the ashes.

vi. Holiday Gift From My Boss

It was an amaryllis
    that came pre-potted
in a little plastic courtroom
    of perlite and peat.
Just add water,
    nothing else—
a life that's self-contained,
    has everything it needs
to construct its colorful ruffle,
    its insignificant scent.
It is the American Dream—
    upward progress to measure
like a stock price.
    Quick results.

vii. Casual Friday

9:35, a fire drill—beeping, beeping—
      as my entire department climbs nine
flights down the designated stairwell
      according to posted evacuation plans,
all of us bound by the practice of single file.

Outside, sales folks gravitate in one cluster
      on the lawn, techies in another.
      It's cold for spring and the poor
main-lobby receptionist is sleeveless.
      She's erasing

her goose bumps by jumping up and down,
      all the while complaining about fake
fire drills, fake bacon bits, fake
      people. On the concrete sidewalk,

colored and molded to simulate brick,
I'm standing, wearing my motorcycle jacket.
      Check the label. It's leather.
      It's genuine.

viii. Post-It Notes

They're my confidants.
To them I entrust my
Anti-Defamation
League ID,
all six digits of

my combination
lock at Work Out World,
my Google password:
Change5. Post-its
are my drill sergeants:

Call Linda! Again,
Call Linda! They're
disposable soldiers
of my mind's advice:
Seize the day. Be the

eyes of kindness. They
absorb the ink of
my thinking—my ball-
point pen writing *Send
Out PowerPoints!* so

hard the next is
embossed *Send Out
PowerPoints!* They stick
to the future gently.
They do not bind. They

approve my useless
doodles: dots, spirals,
grids. They abide the
line by William Carlos
Williams I have

copied: *so much depends...*
On them I've written
large and small: *book on*
Lincoln, meditation,
oil change, duct tape,

flowers. On them I've
written essentials:
bread, water, wine.
Post-its on my mirror.
Post-its on my steering

wheel. Once I wrote
FORGIVE with such
miserable penmanship
the next day I
read it as FORGET!

ix. Promotion

Now I've got what *I* need—
    my raise, my view of the harbor,
my lengthy credenza,
    the oversized bulletin board

    wrapped in dove-gray linen
    on which I've tacked a postcard
of a Chagall—dutiful mule,

peasant who perseveres like I do,
    though sometimes I allow myself
    to stop and contemplate

my oxfords—the oxblood polish
    on the eyelets, the stitches, the rivets,
the steadfast instep, the scuffs.
    I've got to watch my step.

2

Business Trip to Düsseldorf

i: Business Class

Status segregates the Economy
      passengers from us, where it's
champagne before takeoff,
orange juice with swizzle sticks.

The menu's in German.
      Flip-side, English.
Our plush seats recline to beds.
All of us have the same slim
      passport case, the same transatlantic

aspirin, the same telescoping umbrellas,
      the same laptops stashed in ballistic
nylon satchels big enough for one
      million-dollar deal we'll clinch

with practiced nonchalance. All of us
      off to a profitable continent,
where pinstripes are indigenous and striped
      ties, polite.

Concerning the black
spot on the pocket of my white
      shirt, where the ink seeped,
I'm not ashamed. I'm MileagePlus.
      I'm Platinum Elite.

ii: Five-Star Hotel

The wallpaper's sepia weave of sea grass.
The bed's silky quilt and harem of exotic
pillows to choose from—Siberian goose
down, hypoallergenic fiber, Shetland wool.
The mattress promises to memorize
my shape. A silver-plated showerhead
simulates rain. Lotions and boxed soap
populate the bathroom's granite countertop.
And the extendable mirror shuns steam
and magnifies my importance as I shave.

iii: Networking

I zigzag my way through one hundred
forty-seven vendor booths
at the *Druck und Papier* Convention—copier
machines to the west, consumables to the east.
I collect press kits and trade-show giveaways:
thumb drives, key chains, mugs. I network
with sales rep after sales rep, touting product
breakthroughs, until my mind is
a hurt animal flailing its tail,
scraping its spine down the aisle to the exit.
I escape. I fling my wings back to my hotel,
past *Ludwigstrasse,* past *Brükenstrasse.* I stop.
I shudder. I'm worried I didn't have my name
barcode-gunned into the system.

iv. Back in the Hotel Lobby

I watch war in a foreign language,
sich bekriegen, on a big-screen TV.
Blindfolds. Blood. The armored ruckus.

Roadblocks. Tear gas and machine guns
supported by mortars. U.S. ground forces

storming through Bagdad. The enemy,
invisible. Tomorrow I'll breakfast with
Degussa's new CEO, who'll probably brag

about his company's high-performance
catalysts and additives and the slick,

resistant Teflon paint they custom-made
for the walls of Berlin's Holocaust Museum.
Their most successful chemical was,

and always will be, the Zyclon B
that showered Auschwitz.

v. After Dinner with Mr. Müller
from Siemens Nixdorf

It's midnight. I wait alone for the inbound train
        at Alexanderplatz Station.
On the opposite track,
        a guy whose blue button-down shirt is open,
neck to navel.

My God!
With tweezers he's plucking out hairs
        from around his nipples.
And when he finishes,
he tilts a pocket mirror up towards his self-affliction.

Are those dark dots patterning the hankie
in his lap, blood?
        I look away.

His mirror falls to shatter on the platform.
Across the tiles, a hard skitter of slivers.
        I look at him now.
        He looks at me.

vi: Nightmare

The man next in line
    to die
    has made
his backbone stoic.

He wears the ochre
trousers of the fields
    and a white shirt
in colorless surrender.

And though the others
    stand in a huddle
of weeping, he will not

bridle his eyes,
    not make of his hands
a nest of fret.

The persecution squad
clicks to attention,
    rifles primed.
This is the art of defiance,
    the refusal to cower
when power turns
    brutal.
    I am next in line.

vii: Kunstpalast Museum

My client wants to buy me postcards—
    Dürer's *St. Jerome in His Study*,
squinting in disenfranchised light.

    And Cranach's *Expulsion*:
panicked Adam, no fig leaf, no clouds,
    just the shameful snake.

He wants to buy me a money clip
    because I gave him a significant
    discount on our patented software.

He wants to buy me a poster of angels robbed
    of their bodies, a poster of
    Jesus from whose rib flows blood.

I can't resist offering him two
crucifix bookmarks: two
    for the price of one.

viii: Weekending in Wannbach

This is the very town
where my grandpa once worked a store:
    pewter tableware,
pewter tankards, goblets, steins.

In the Mühlhäuser tavern, I order
    a glass of Gewürztraminer,
a salad of sauerkraut and beets.

My grandpa had saved enough
    Reichsmarks to buy
a steerage ticket on the SS Exeter
    to New York. It was 1939,
the year young men hung
from butcher hooks at Buchenwald.

For dessert I order wafers and a shot
of German schnapps
    to give my lips a smack.

ix: On the Way to the Airport

I ask my taxi driver to stop at a scenic pull off
so I can look at the Ruhr River rapids
and wonder about rockslides, steep ravines.

A gray boulder batters the backwash and the froth.

Which god is it who decides whether
to strand the salmon or grant them passage?
Whether or not to let the beavers have their dam?

Did my grandpa leave his boothee s' imprints
in that bank muck, kneel down,
dip his hands in, drink?

3

Business Trip to Las Vegas

i. Representing the Company at a Job Fair

I sit by a wall socket, charge my phone.
How thirsty I am, having (for six hours,
seven minutes) apprenticed my lips
to the grin-of-a-thousand *YESes*—another
eager applicant I'm not pleased with.

> In comes a guy wearing black
> cycling tights, a yellow helmet,
> and Nikes (xenon blue).
> He's dropping off a package
> at the Nielsen Company booth,
> where I'd once opened my
> briefcase filled with innovation
> and my best intentions.
> Even I could feel messianic,
> carrying a satchel with *DELIVER ME!*
> stenciled on the flap.

At the refreshment table everything is
political. The spout of the silver urn lets
hot water chart its hopeful flow. I open
a bag of herbal tea—assertive, self-effacing.

ii. At the Bellagio Coffee Shop

I've got a coffee headache
from rehashing every
        saleable complaint,
but when that woman whose sunken
key ring I retrieved from the deep end

        of Caesars Palace's pool
comes in and sits beside me
        at the counter, clinking her bangle
bracelets so they tango,
        my headache fades.

So I crank my brightness up a notch and go
incendiary. Hello infidelity. Hello
        to her skin so pale it doesn't belong
in nature. Hello to her hair,
        the yellow hubbub of the sun.

She unfolds a paper napkin,
        takes off her glasses to clean them.
Just then her trusting eyes
        seem—God, I don't know—so
        beautiful and tragic.

She slips off one spike-heeled shoe,
        fingers the fringe of her short skirt.
I'm wondering if her thighs might be
        unbridled by her windfall at the slots.

It's momentary happiness I fathom
        in the outback of her eyes.
Honey, I say, *please pass the sweetener.*

Anything else you need? she asks.
I wink.

iii. Postcard From Nevada

Two business meetings: one bright
as geodes, little crystal facets dazzling; the other,
twisted as tumbleweed and thorny scrub.

Two-hour hike in Canyon de Chelly, all cliffs
and abysses in a desert style of light. Hotel lobby
with art show by children from the Pueblo:

thinly penciled cactus, its spindly ribs; photo
of a cliché vulture on a cliché fence; dry-brushed
coyote, water-colored brown, sick of howling at the moon.

iv: To Kill Time Before My Red-Eye Flight

I visit a Goodwill store, where time has
dropped off a box of books. *Philosophy*, it reads,
though it's mostly cookbooks,

some Hobbes and Socrates mixed in.
Time has taken all the paintings away,
leaving a stack of empty frames,

gold-leafed and needing polish.
I pick up a cast iron Abraham Lincoln,
a mother of pearl and ivory inlaid

cigarette box, a forty-dollar hunting knife.
On a pink marble pedestal there is
a statue of Saint Anthony, who makes me

think of lost things—like our family piano.
There is no piano here, but on top
of the piano bench there's a tattered

leather bible. Of course I pick it up, hold it
in both my hands, open to the unbegrudging
comfort of worn-in prayers.

v: On the Red-Eye

I tilt the seatback screen.
On the armrest controls I fidget
the volume six clicks up, watch
the in-flight movie about the human

     cannonball who fell
     in love with the acrobat,
     but she loves the man
     who trains the monkeys.

It's the circus—everybody is in bed
with somebody else. The ticket taker
succumbs to the scent of cedar
sawdust in the lion tamer's hair.

     The lion tamer fancies
     the Portuguese contortionist,
     whose job it is to dislocate
     the status quo.

4

Business Trip to Orlando

i: Presentation at the Digital Imaging Conference

What if the bulb of my projector blows
and static jams the microphone until it bleats

> like sheep? Or my throat
> gets parched and the pitcher
> on the lectern is empty
> and the engine of my lungs
> heats the air around me
> till my forehead sweats,

my armpits unleash their black
dogs, the stack of handouts I've so carefully

> prepared spontaneously combusts,
> and it's up to me to beat
> the flames with a broom?
> What if everyone laughs
> at my struggle to find words
> that will be as crucial as those

of the pilot (*Mayday! Mayday!*) recorded
in the black box recovered from the wreckage.

ii: Protégé

Yes. I've decided that she will give
the keynote at the next
Digital Imaging Conference in Orlando.

Up there alone on stage
in her fitted red business suit,
she won't be any pale gardenia just picked

from a cut-glass bowl. No. She will be
the wunderkind without a wedding ring.
In front of hundreds of executives

keen on sharpening their wit,
she'll rouse their full attention.
She'll bring them to their knees.

iii: After Lunch with a Client
at the Tampa Museum of Art

I decide to tour the special
exhibit, for which Gabriel Orozco
has made a scroll
of the New York City
white-pages phone book
by cutting out
peoples' names from
their ten-digit listings,
ditching the names,
skimming archival glue
on the back of each
anonymous column of numbers
before pressing it down
on a roll of tissue-thin kozo
paper, so eighteen million
names of the metropolitan
population are contained
in one document
twenty-five continuous
meters long, of which
only a segment at a time
can be displayed
in the plateglass case,
towards which the lens
of the surveillance
camera is pointed,
counting us visitors
frame by frame,
saving us, pixel by pixel,
like digital lint.

iv: Disney World

Isn't profit equal
to the throughput
of tourists, multiplied
by every thrill that's
hell-bent or neck-deep
in plummeting,

plus souvenir pirate money, plus fool's gold, plus
jawbreakers, plus all-day suckers, plus chainsaws,
plus the pitiless, perpetual wood chipper, as one
after another swamp of old-growth cypress falls

down the chute,
leaving only the stumps'
concentric accounting
of short-sightedness
and hubris: *at least*
it's creating jobs.

v: Day Off in Key West

The wind picks up
    the tide, puts down the tide,
embellishing the shoreline with shells,
    each one having something
missing: the other half, the lip,
    the aperture, the whorl.

Hundreds of horseflies swarm
    one piece of carrageen seaweed.
I get into my rented kayak, do the slow
    work of paddling around
the mangroves that hold Key West
    together by a lock bolt. Time

to dive in, snorkel around anemones,
    undulating hydra, sponges, the kelp.

The ocean's most loyal employee is
    the horseshoe crab, which was here
before the stars spoke in zodiacs,
    before office work became
one giant island we derived.

5

Business Trip to Richmond, Where I Grew Up

i. At the Podium

I shine my laser pointer,
the red blip tracking trend lines: the x-axis
of time; y, customer satisfaction.
        I tell them success is
        no longer about money
but credit—give it to the new unqualified:

inner-city single moms with mortgages;
students with their part-time jobs;
        widows, pressed hard.
        Rein in, I tell them,
their grace period to thirty days,
rip them off with sky-high interest rates
        on their revolving debt.

Afterwards, I look out at Franklin Street,
        the brownstone storefront
        where my grandpa sold belts
of cloth, buttons, suspenders, top hats
he'd sometimes let me open
        and collapse.

I drive to James River Park, follow the trails
        I used to follow
through cabbage grass and sassafras,
through kudzu, as I searched for the crown
        of a puffball mushroom   could stomp,
        let out its smell—
sulfur and ugly.

ii. Workability

When we were kids,
my brother would reach across
    the dinner table to my plate,
    grab my dessert,
shove the cupcake in his mouth,
    wolf it down.

Once I gave him a popsicle so cold
I knew (and he knew, too)
    it would stick to his tongue.
Then he locked me in the tool shed—
    dark, cramped retribution.

I have a photograph in which I'm five,
    my brother six. It must be
Virginia Beach in the background.
We're wearing matching navy shorts,
    matching polos, matching cotton
    socks rolled down,
matching canvas tennis shoes
we tied with matching double bows.
    We are a year, a month, a week, a day
apart, one entity
    our parents called *the boys*.

Sometimes I forget I have a brother.
    We never talk; though talking
brings a bonus, an upside.

iii. The Room We Shared

Our father's six-by-ten-foot map
of the world that used to hang
over his desk in Army Headquarters in Manila
was pasted across our bedroom wall.
I slept with my head near Malaysia.
My brother slept under Brazil.
The colors of that map were coded
by elevation, same colors our mother
used to decorate our room.
And so, my orange bedspread matched
the Himalayas. Our sheets were white

as Antarctica was white.
The curtains were the same
yellow as the Russian tundra.
Some nights our father would tell us
stories about the map—the prick holes
where he'd pushed pins in to chart
the progress of destroyers in the Pacific.
A circle penciled around Nagasaki.
Another circle, Hiroshima. Shipping
routes in big red arcs from port to port.
A stain, he said, where he'd coughed

coffee over the coast of Madagascar
not far from the blot of where
he'd slapped a mosquito dead.
Time changed the names of things.
Transjordan ditched the *Trans* to be just Jordan.
The French Sahara stopped answering
to France. Belgian Congo wasn't Belgian
anymore. Between my brother's twin bed
and my twin bed, there was always
an imaginary buffer zone, starting
at Tanganyika, ending at the closet door.

iv. Work Ethic

Even on Sundays my father worked
    in the garage—honing, oiling
the pruning sheers, adjusting
    the demeanor of the rakes,
standing them straight as soldiers,
    making them stay.
At his downtown office I'd sit
    and swivel the swivel chair, slice
envelopes with the paper-cutter guillotine.
    When his very pretty secretary came in
with his cup of oolong tea,
    she always said, *I hope you like it.*
Then he'd take off his glasses,
    put his face in his hands.
Sometimes, in his side chair, I opened
    my three-ring notebook on my lap
to lick and stick onto loose-leaf paper
    my reinforcements.

v. Driving Past Kessler's Farm
on the Way to the Richmond Airport

One summer I worked that farm,
lugging fifty-pound salt blocks
to the pasture for livestock to lick.

> I bailed barley.
> I chased away
> grackles that had
> ransacked the trash.

In the orchards—the gnarly
branches of apple trees: Jersey Mac,
Jonamac, Dorset Golden.

Down the dirt road to the barn I'd trudge
with a knapsack and paper bags to fill
the farmer's commitment to cider.

Sometimes I'd scrub (down on
hands and knees) the brown-coat
off the linoleum.

Nights I'd sleep on a lumpy horsehair
mattress in the room over the porch,
my sheets coarse as feedbags.

> And wasn't I
> happy, so happy,
> in the mornings
> to wake up and run?

6

Re-Evaluation

i. Nature Revises Its Business Plan

It's summer. Q3.
Time for a midyear adjustment.
Time to remark on my accomplishments.
Some, like sunflowers, are too
haughty for their own good,
too proud of their core of seedsong.
Some are spiders.
Some are raindrops.
I assign to each of my direct
reports a developmental goal.
This time of year I usually
revise their milestones.
I water my garden nine to five,
color-code the marigolds.
Bees profit from the nectar,
its assets and liabilities.
Thistles spike in the franchise.
No one has to teach leaf buds to negotiate
or roots to collaborate with topsoil
or with rot.

ii. Self-Assessment

I am a swarm
of logic, a force
with a spiritual
center marked
by a spire, more
passionate than
average, attentive
with a limerick's
sense of humor,
methodical as a
lifeguard, even
during rain. I am
a good writer, able
to organize words
by their appetite.
I focus on the big
picture. I delegate.
I know how to
assess, on the x-axis,
someone's skill, and
on the y, willingness.
I know when to say
less than necessary,
when to rev energy, as
if the air was caffeine.

iii. Inner Workings

Happy is always tinged with something else—
    for example, the thankful-kind-of-happy
after flying through terrible turbulence

from a convention in Berlin back to Chicago,
    where touchdown brings the whoosh
as the wing flaps lift.

And wasn't I vain-happy at the company-sponsored
    Blood Drive, when it took me seven point
five minutes, and the CEO lying on

the donation table next to me eleven
    minutes to pump out an A-positive pint?
I won't let myself be proud-happy about

my Best in Sales trophy, but I was vengeful-
    happy when my old boss, who was great
at hailing taxis (but low on doling out

bonuses) got transferred to the miserable
    Division of Statistics. I believe in the laugh-
at-myself-happy, like when, on account

of blizzard, I decided to stay home, consulting
    my driveway, shoveling three feet of snow
that kept on blowing (*goddamnit*) back in my face.

iv. Information

I'm drowning in information
like I did in college, when I brimmed
with coefficients and every civil
engineering fact. Trussed
and buttressed I was,

>   until my mind shut its mouth.
>   First semester freshman year
>   the outcome of two student
>   suicides left every third-to-tenth-

floor dorm-room window bolted
shut. Now it's record-breaking
rainfall, pipelines, and the distant
fires of the refineries,
category fours in the Gulf,

>   and Greenland's ice sheet, declining.
>   That same semester, I found
>   a baby robin in the quad,
>   took it in my backpack to my

dorm room, where I ripped up
old calculus homework to pad
a nest in a Florsheim shoebox,
fed that robin water, eyedrop-
by-eyedrop, until it died.

v. Customer Service

I am the lathe
turning work
into newel-post. I am
a machine with moving parts:
ball bearings, gears,
the ratchet of the best
available answer at the best
available time,
the most important
lever, the influence
brought to bear. Even if
the sale is untamable,
even if the pitch has
lurched to fury,
I will be patient.
I will classify.
I will say, *I don't know.*
I will say, *I'll find out.*
I'll never invent, nor pretend.
Even over the phone,
with no facial feedback,
my voice always carries
a grin. No monotone.
Always full timbre.
I am Customer Service, the man
who builds the brand.

vi. Teamwork

One team member is always
the rickety bridge.
Another: fill material.
Another: expansion joint.
I rely on Cynthia for seminal
potential to counter
Mark, who siphons off
everybody's excitement in these
brainstorming sessions,
as I try to balance things: no one
daunted, no pummel-down,
no crosstalk. I've assigned
a timekeeper so we stay
on track. I've set
the ground rules for myself—
One: no looking at my cell.
Two: no getting lost again in the blue
eyes of Monica, the audio-visual
technician with her clicker
and her tight, crisp blouse. Three:
don't call Jianyu the name
of the other Chinese guy.
I say *bottom line it* if someone gets
persistent. All day long I magic
marker key points on the whiteboard.
All day long I wait
for happy hour. I rarely think
outside the box. My pat answer:
connect the dots. It's a good
meeting if I challenge more
pat answers than I give.

vii. Firefly, Moon, Rain, Wall Street

The job of a thousand fireflies in a field
      is to synchronize their blink,
little biological oscillators that they are.
The moon's job is to regulate
      the waves on a twice-daily basis,
to dole out paychecks monthly.
Rain's job is, in fact, reliable,
      falling like glitter
on the hemlocks' limbs.
The job of Wall Street is to arise
      from the gutter of worldly debris,
like downtown worms arise to meet
      their own undoings on a sidewalk—
      someone's shoe the final blow.

7

Shaking Off My Expectations

i. Groundwork

Blood worms stunned
by the sun
can't help but
retreat back down.
Moths can't
help stammering.
The humming-
birds lunge
their slender tongues
into the blooms
of the *Epiphyllum* cacti
that widen into fire.
I'm shaking off
my expectations of
anything abiding.
How quickly
a grasshopper will
sheathe its wings, renege
on its attachment
to a stem. Tomorrow
the pollen that yellows
paving slates will
wash away in rain.

ii. Exit Strategy

So many ways for an employee
to leave a company—
two weeks' notice, hasty layoffs,
an entire department phasing out.
So many ways for seeds to leave—
exploding from a pod, carried off
by a parachute of uplift and fluff.
I left my college job with a simple
I quit! No more stacking
mulch sacks in the tool shed,
no more raking or yanking out rampant
maple saplings rooted in the privet hedge.
I said *So long!* to the squirrels scrabbling
against the oak bark, wandering in
and out of trellises. *So long!*
to the marks of mower wheels
that used to corrugate that lawn.

iii. When Is Enough Enough

My final summer in the corporate world,
the reservoirs were low
all over town. Signs posted:
Ban On Watering.
Sprinklers and hoses, *verboten,*
so the copper beech in my yard, losing
leaves, an arid rattling on the asphalt.

Ants came inside the house,
searching for water. Birds
pecked at the melons for a sip.

For thirty years in Corporate
America, I kept telling myself
there are always more
spreadsheets to shred into the nest egg
of the 401(k), always more
sandbags to tilt against risk;
so I kept working, honing
my expertise, reducing
the unequivocal jargon
of the consumer world
to data points. *I hate my job,*

though I kept it, comforting myself
with a good salary, some good
clients, agreeable with sound-absorbing
the walls of each other, including the dubious
cubicles of our winterized temperaments.

I had problem clients, too,
for whom I emptied the facts
and tatters of my monologue.
Silence is my tool, my interlude,
my leeway. Even still, my mind hovers
ever-watchful at falcon height.

iv. Fired

They call it *downsizing.*
They don't give a reason.
They don't have to.
      Good riddance to my boss
and my boss's boss
and his boss for whom
      I'm just another scrap of winter.
So long Sandy, I say
to the administrative assistant
      who stands, hands behind her back,
watching me empty
the wreckage of my desk drawer—
      safety pin, collar stay,
the red thumbtack I used
to post the photo of my team
      on a sun-struck Boston duckboat.
I toss the handkerchief
from Japan Airlines. I toss
      fourteen years of budget spreadsheets,
the lithium battery whose life
has been worn down.
      I put on my coat, decide
to take the freight elevator down,
sneak out the back,
            piss loudly on the new
aluminum skin of the toolshed
in the office park,
      leave long yellow-wet graffiti,
making a statement, like migrating
geese do when one flies
      out of compliance with the mutually
agreed-upon "V."

v. Worktable for My Home Office

I measure, cut two-by-fours
        to brace the table's corners,
bolt steel wheels to every leg,
use an ergonomic hammer

(all stronghold and gung ho)
to attach the four-ply birchwood top,
        but every nail I pound goes

wrong. I have to slip the rip claw
        under the bent-down head,
tug, and readjust how hard I tug
and with what intention. Who knows
        what knot crooked it,
and under that knot, what trauma,
        and under that trauma, whose

responsibility? When I pull out
        nails, at least one is skittish,
persistent, and in the frictioned
        heat of its letting go
tight-grained wood, it speaks out

in a high-pitched voice.
        All I can do is listen, as if
it were the voice of shame.

vi. At a Hardware Store

I buy some rough-whiskered rope, sturdy-
in-its-strands rope to lift a mainsail,
to lift a jib. Rope good enough for lashing.
Rope perfect for practicing: fisherman's
knot, reef knot, square knot to bind everyone
to everyone else, grapple hitch that takes
me everywhere I mean to go, clove hitch
that forever keeps approaching reconciliation.
I even like to make up knots: the un-
assailable knot, the not-me knot.
A decent length of twine is all I need to loop
a slew of slip knots. One tug from both ends
at once: human undoing.

vii. Final Refusal

My old dog refuses water,
refuses food. When I take him
for a walk, he lifts his leg
as if he has to piss,
though there's no piss in him
whose withers quiver,
whose heart swells
visible between the ribs.
He doesn't perk his ears
at two bickering wrens,
doesn't sniff the unsavory
sidewalk cracks, doesn't
even yelp as we pass
a playground, the shiny slides
and the wind making the slung
seats of swings sway
with no one in them.
Nor does he look up at the valiant
fluttering of apple blossom's
pink confetti. It's just
the pitiful click of claws
on concrete, a slack leash,
his scuffed nose taking
in the air oppressed
with the forecast of snow.

viii. On the Cold Side of Things

I used to love the rain-freeze
that made playgrounds glisten,
and the white columns of factory
smoke eking into ether,

and the naked branches
networked and projected
onto sun-struck walls,
and the red shock of holly berries
against snow. I used to watch

my dad's car submerged
above its grillwork,
the fence upended by drifts,
the daggers of stalactites

slung from gutters. Today,
zero on the thermometer
fills me with resignation.
Or is it bereavement? Is it
snow forces me to know

I'm mortal, no longer
skating the snow crust,
no longer begging
the surface for slide?

ix. Driving to My First Day of Therapy

A therapist might be a pry bar
to open up the past again,
focusing searchlights on my apocrypha,
the untidy, strived-for milestones,

the scarf and gloves of my heart's cold hungers.
Some days it was easy for me to be steamed
into froth by an argument with a co-worker
over artificial sweeteners. December
is such a gaudy time of year. Poinsettias
on the window sills at Starbucks reaching

their leafy peak and the Christmas cactus
on the counter showing wounds.
We're all wounded in some way.
That frowning tattooed guy who,

as we're inching forward in line, keeps
a three-foot gap is wounded.
And the patchouli-scented girl, wearing
a paisley skirt and kerchief, wounded.
Sometimes I get stuck in the tinsel-flicker
of decision. Which brew to choose?

Sumatra. Java. Kona. Or which therapist?
Surely the one I've chosen won't be contemptuous
of poetry or anything wispy, anything
that flutters in the webbing of the breath.

x. Volunteer

I try teaching writing
      at minimum security, put a red check mark
in the margin of an inmate's yellow

legal pad, beside *and the makeshift*
      plywood shelf with cans of corned beef
hash came crashing down.

I write *nice details* beside the four iambs of
a burlap sack of black-eyed peas.
      Thanks, he says, then stands up, points between
the bars to the prison commons, and continues—

Those are my tulips. My azaleas. I mulch that bed.
      I wonder if he's conning me. Maybe all writing is
a con, a ploy to make your readers love you.

When I was a kid, I slept with the window open,
      even in winter. I wanted to hear the sirens
and the backfires. I took notes about the urgent

sermons of the crows, and the carcasses
      of cars at the scrapyard, and the one-armed man
raking steaming asphalt into highway holes.

Is it hardship I'm attracted to? Or hazard?
      Or chance? I don't know what my student is
incarcerated for, and I don't ask.

xi. Moderate Risk

I don't buy lottery tickets.
   I don't believe in squandering,
or that money begets happiness.
   But from the gutter I gather up
losses other people have thrown away—
   the ones the sun has
sucked the brightest colors from.
   Or was it acid rain? Or was it tears?

xii. On a Park Bench, Boston Commons

Didn't the asphalt on Tremont Street begin
as something panting and organic? Even
the fountain, drained for winter, is ready
for a subsequent career as a pigeon's picking ground

of popcorn, my shredded resume, hope.
In college I mopped classrooms.
After that I marketed seeds (heirloom tomatoes),
wore a white paper hat to manage a failing

Dairy Queen, sold silicone chips—the best
megahertz to ramp the dance of diodes.
Part-time Customer Service Rep. C++
Programmer. Trade Magazine Editor.

Market Research Director. VP, Strategy
and Analytics. Before the Big Bang
revamped the universe, the sun was
random gasses. Now it's working

overtime, colliding isotopes of hydrogen,
while I sit on a bench (a recycled plastic bench)
made from soda bottles that changed their job.
Everything used to work as something else.

Acknowledgments

Thanks to the National Endowment for the Arts for a fellowship in poetry that helped make the writing possible. Grateful acknowledgment is made to the following journals and anthologies where these poems first appeared, sometimes as earlier versions, sometimes under different titles:

3 Nations Anthology: "At a Hardware Store"
Aurorean: "Fired," "Driving Past Kessler's Farm, On the Way to the Richmond Airport"
Borderlands: "Post-It Notes"
Coffee Poems Anthology: "Driving to My First Day of Therapy"
Concho River Review: "Memo from the CEO"
Dash: "Firefly, Moon, Rain, Wall Street"
Exit 7: "After Lunch with a Client at the Tampa Museum of Art"
Forgotten Women Anthology: "Smoking Area"
Ice Cream Anthology: "At the Bellagio Coffee Shop"
Into the Teeth of the Wind: "Promotion"
One: "Groundwork"
Oyez Review: "Business Class"
Pedestal Magazine: "Disney World"
Poetry East: "Networking"
Potomac Review: "Work Ethic"
Riverwind: "Day Off in Key West"
Sahara: "Business Trip to Richmond," "Nature Revises Its Business Plan"
Salamander: "Kunstpalast Museum"
Third Wednesday: "On the Way to the Airport"
Two Hawks Quarterly: "On the Cold Side of Things," "Smoking"

I am grateful to my friends in The Workshop for Publishing Poets, who helped me hone these poems, and especially to Barbara Helfgott-Hyett (friend, mentor, poet-sister) for her poetic know-how and her advice that I write about the working world I know.

Special thanks to my employers—Bitstream, Lyra, Forrester Research—for providing income and experience. Special thanks to Charles L. for teaching me to be a feature-story writer and for sending me all over the world to cover conferences, and to Ted S., who saw in me a leader. Thanks to my work colleagues who graced my workdays.

I would not have written this book without the love, respect, wisdom, and support of my wife, Leslie. Others I would like to thank are Patrick Singleton for the back cover photo and Gena, Helen, Jeff, Kitty, and others whose friendship and wisdom sustain me.

About FutureCycle Press

FutureCycle Press is dedicated to publishing lasting English-language poetry books, chapbooks, and anthologies in both print-on-demand and Kindle ebook formats. Founded in 2007 by long-time independent editor/publishers and partners Diane Kistner and Robert S. King, the press incorporated as a nonprofit in 2012. A number of our editors are distinguished poets and writers in their own right, and we have been actively involved in the small press movement going back to the early seventies.

The FutureCycle Poetry Book Prize and honorarium is awarded annually for the best full-length volume of poetry we publish in a calendar year. Introduced in 2013, our Good Works projects are anthologies devoted to issues of universal significance, with all proceeds donated to a related worthy cause. Our Selected Poems series highlights contemporary poets with a substantial body of work to their credit; with this series we strive to resurrect work that has had limited distribution and is now out of print.

We are dedicated to giving all of the authors we publish the care their work deserves, making our catalog of titles the most diverse and distinguished it can be, and paying forward any earnings to fund more great books.

We've learned a few things about independent publishing over the years. We've also evolved a unique, resilient publishing model that allows us to focus mainly on vetting and preserving for posterity poetry collections of exceptional quality without becoming overwhelmed with bookkeeping and mailing, fundraising activities, or taxing editorial and production "bubbles." To find out more about what we are doing, come see us at www.futurecycle.org.

The FutureCycle Poetry Book Prize

All full-length volumes of poetry published by FutureCycle Press in a calendar year are considered for the annual FutureCycle Poetry Book Prize. This allows us to consider each submission on its own merits, outside of the context of a contest. Too, the judges see the finished book, which will have benefitted from the beautiful book design and strong editorial gloss we are famous for.

The book ranked the best in judging is announced as the prize-winner in the subsequent year. There is no fixed monetary award; instead, the winning poet receives an honorarium of 20% of the total net royalties from all poetry books and chapbooks the press sold online in the year the winning book was published. The winner is also accorded the honor of being on the panel of judges for the next year's competition; all judges receive copies of all contending books to keep for their personal library.

9 781942 371618